I0814231

NORTH AMERICAN FIELD GUIDES

WILDFLOWERS

Carla Mooney

An Imprint of Abdo Reference | abdobooks.com

CONTENTS

WHAT ARE WILDFLOWERS?

Wildflowers are beautiful, colorful plants that grow in nature without needing to be planted or cared for by people. They can be found in forests, fields, and meadows. They can even be found along roadsides. Wildflowers come in many different shapes, sizes, and colors. Some are small and delicate, while others can grow quite tall. They may bloom in the spring, summer, or fall, depending on the kind of wildflower. In some regions a few wildflowers may even bloom during the winter months.

Wildflowers are important for the environment. They provide food for pollinators such as bees, butterflies, and hummingbirds. Pollinators move from flower to flower to feed on the nectar. Pollen from the flower collects on their bodies. It brushes off on other flowers they visit. Many flowers need this pollen from other flowers to reproduce. The flowers can then produce seeds that will grow into new plants.

Wherever wildflowers grow, they send out deep roots that hold soil in place, reducing erosion from wind or rain. Wildflowers also provide shelter and a place to reproduce for many species of insects and other wildlife. When wildflowers die, the flowers' leaves and stems fall to the ground and decompose, returning nutrients to the soil. These nutrients improve the soil quality and provide a healthy environment for growing new plants.

IDENTIFYING WILDFLOWERS

Scientists estimate that there are more than 20,000 wildflower species in North America. These species are divided into groups called families. There are many different families of wildflowers, including aster, poppy, rose, and violet.

Wildflowers from the same family share common traits. These include color, size, and shape of flowers and leaves; how tall they grow; and where they grow. For example, some wildflowers grow in dry, sandy soil, while other wildflowers thrive in wet, swampy conditions.

In this book, wildflowers are described according to their appearance. This includes the arrangement of leaves and the color and structure of the flowers. When identifying wildflowers, it is helpful to also note the following characteristics:

- Size: The average height or length of a plant.
- North American Range: The geographic area in which the flower grows.
- Habitat: The type of environment in which the flower thrives.
- Bloom Period: The months during which the flower usually blooms.

LEAF STRUCTURE AND ARRANGEMENT

Wildflower leaves have different structures and arrangements. There are two main types of structures. A simple leaf is undivided, which means it has a single blade. A compound leaf has separate blades called leaflets.

There are three major types of arrangements. Opposite leaves grow in pairs from the same point on the stem. Alternating leaves each grow from a single point, with each leaf a little higher on the stem than the last one. And in the whorled leaf pattern, three or more leaves grow from a single point.

HOW TO USE THIS BOOK

Tab shows the wildflower category.

ASTER FAMILY

COMMON DANDELION

(TARAXACUM OFFICINALE)

The wildflower's common name appears here.

...dandelion grows across North America from ...uced to North America from ...ow flower head surrounded ...ch flower is about 1.5 inches ...omes from the French phrase *dent d*... ...s "lion's tooth." When broken, dandelion stems release a milky liquid. The flower's long, toothed leaves are used in salads and soups.

HOW TO SPOT

Size: 2 to 18 inches (5 to 46 cm) tall

North American Range: Throughout Canada, the United States, and Mexico

Habitat: Meadows, lawns, and roadsides

Bloom Period: March to September

How to Spot boxes give information about the wildflower's size, range, habitat, and bloom period.

WILDFLOWER OR WEED?

Some wildflowers grow where they are not wanted. Wildflowers that spread quickly in lawns, gardens, and similar places are sometimes called weeds. Many people consider the dandelion a weed because it spreads uninvited across carefully tended lawns. However, a weed ...n may be a beautiful wildflower to another.

14

Sidebars provide additional information about the topic.

OMMON SUNFLOWE

LIANTHUS ANNUUS)

The wildflower's scientific name appears here.

common sunflower grows on a tall, hairy stem. Each m splits into branches that grow several bright yellow wers with 17 to 40 petals. The flower's petals surround ark, reddish-brown flower head. Each flower is about o 5 inches (8 to 13 cm) wide. The sunflower's head moves face the sun. Its toothed leaves are broad and either egg heart shaped. Sunflowers produce edible seeds that are so used to make cooking oil.

This paragraph gives information about the wildflower.

HOW TO SPOT

Size: 2 to 13 feet (0.6 to 4 m) tall
North American Range: Alaska, Canada, and the United States, south to Costa Rica
Habitat: Prairies, roadsides, and fields
Bloom Period: June to November

Images show the wildflower.

FUN FACT

The Hopi people have traditionally used sunflowers to create dyes for use in crafting baskets and dying wool and cotton.

Fun Facts give interesting information about wildflowers.

15

GOLDEN ALEXANDERS

(ZIZIA AUREA)

Golden alexanders is a bright yellow wildflower. Its small, yellow flowers bloom in clusters that look like tiny umbrellas. Each flower has five petals and five sepals. A flower cluster grows up to 2.5 inches (6.4 cm) wide. Its green stems are tall and sturdy, with compound leaves that have an egg shape with jagged edges. Leaves grow alternately on the stem. Golden alexanders bloom in spring, bringing color to fields before many other flowers appear.

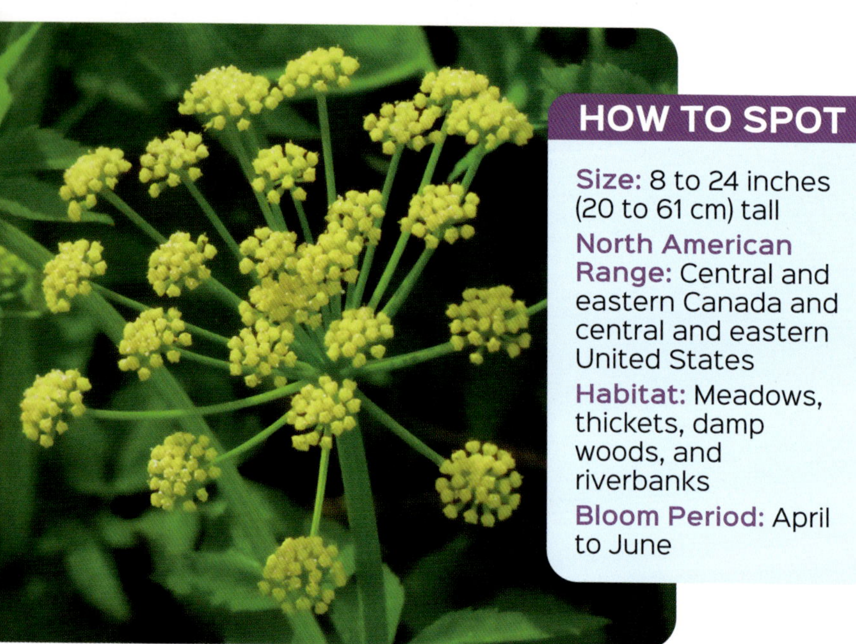

HOW TO SPOT

Size: 8 to 24 inches (20 to 61 cm) tall

North American Range: Central and eastern Canada and central and eastern United States

Habitat: Meadows, thickets, damp woods, and riverbanks

Bloom Period: April to June

LEAF SHAPES

Wildflower leaves come in different shapes. Some are shaped like an arrow or lance. Other leaves are long and narrow. Some leaves are shaped like a heart, while other leaves are long and oval shaped. Leaves may also be somewhat circular or even diamond shaped. A leaf's edges vary as well. Some are toothed, or jagged. Others are lobed, which means they have rounded or pointed segments that extend from the main leaf.

SPOTTED WATER HEMLOCK

(CICUTA MACULATA)

Spotted water hemlock is a tall plant that has small, white flowers that bloom in clusters. Each cluster measures about 3 inches (8 cm) wide. The plant has bright green compound leaves that have an arrow shape and toothed edges. Leaves grow alternately on the stem. The smooth, hollow stem can be purple or green with purple streaks.

HOW TO SPOT

Size: 3 to 6.5 feet (0.9 to 2 m) tall

North American Range: Throughout North America, from northern Canada to Mexico

Habitat: Wet meadows, thickets, wetlands, and swamps

Bloom Period: June to September

FUN FACT

Water hemlock is one of the most poisonous plants in North America. Even a small amount can be very dangerous to humans and animals if eaten.

CARROT FAMILY

WILD CARROT *(DAUCUS CAROTA)*

Wild carrot, also known as Queen Anne's lace, is a tall, delicate plant with long, fern-like leaves. Large clusters of white flowers form a flat, umbrella-like shape. As many as 1,000 flowers with tiny petals make up the clusters, which are about 3 to 5 inches (8 to 13 cm) across. In the center of each cluster is a tiny purplish flower. When crushed, the leaves smell like carrots. However, contact with the leaves can irritate skin.

HOW TO SPOT

Size: 1 to 3.5 feet (0.3 to 1.1 m) tall
North American Range: Across the continental United States and parts of Canada
Habitat: Fields, meadows, and roadsides
Bloom Period: May to October

FUN FACT

Wild carrot reproduces when seeds are spread by the wind and carried by animals to new areas.

WILD PARSNIP *(PASTINACA SATIVA)*

Wild parsnip is a tall plant with bright yellow flowers that bloom in wide, flat clusters. Each flower has five petals. The flower cluster grows to about 3 to 8 inches (8 to 20 cm) wide. The plant has green, compound leaves with 5 to 15 egg-shaped, toothed leaflets. The plant's root is a parsnip, a root vegetable that people can eat when grown in gardens. However, because the wild parsnip looks like the toxic plants poison hemlock and water hemlock, wild parsnip should not be eaten. Contact with the plant's leaves, stems, and flowers can irritate the skin, especially when the affected skin is exposed to sunlight.

HOW TO SPOT

Size: 2 to 5 feet (0.6 to 1.5 m) tall

North American Range: Alaska, most of Canada and the United States (except Florida, Georgia, and Alabama), Cuba, the Dominican Republic, and Haiti

Habitat: Meadows and roadsides

Bloom Period: May to June

BLACK-EYED SUSAN

(RUDBECKIA HIRTA)

The black-eyed susan is a biennial plant that blooms in its second year. Its daisy-like flowers have 8 to 20 golden-yellow petals and brownish-black centers. Each flower grows approximately 2 to 3 inches (5 to 8 cm) wide. It has scattered oval leaves covered with fuzzy hairs. The nectar from the flowers attracts many butterflies, bees, and other insects. The black-eyed susan thrives in full sunlight and grows well in various soils.

FUN FACT

The black-eyed susan is the state flower of Maryland.

HOW TO SPOT

Size: 1 to 3 feet (0.3 to 0.9 m) tall

North American Range: Throughout Canada, the continental United States, and Mexico

Habitat: Prairies, plains, meadows, and open fields

Bloom Period: June to October

BLANKETFLOWER

(GAILLARDIA PULCHELLA)

The blanketflower has pinkish-red petals with yellow tips. Six to 18 ray-like petals surround a flower head like a pinwheel. Each petal has three lobes. A flower about 1.5 to 3 inches (4 to 8 cm) wide grows on each stem. Its leaves grow alternately on the stem. Leaves are oblong with smooth or toothed edges. The flower has been used in medicine, and researchers are studying it for use in cancer prevention.

HOW TO SPOT

Size: 1 to 2 feet (0.3 to 0.6 m) tall

North American Range: Alaska, Ontario and Quebec in Canada, most of the continental United States, and Mexico

Habitat: Sandy plains and deserts

Bloom Period: May to July

ASTER FAMILY

COMMON DANDELION

(TARAXACUM OFFICINALE)

The common dandelion grows across North America from spring to early fall. It was introduced to North America from Europe. The dandelion has a yellow flower head surrounded by many bright yellow petals. Each flower is about 1.5 inches (4 cm) wide. The flower's name comes from the French phrase *dent de lion,* which means "lion's tooth." When broken, dandelion stems release a milky liquid. The flower's long, toothed leaves are used in salads and soups.

HOW TO SPOT

Size: 2 to 18 inches (5 to 46 cm) tall

North American Range: Throughout Canada, the United States, and Mexico

Habitat: Meadows, lawns, and roadsides

Bloom Period: March to September

WILDFLOWER OR WEED?

Some wildflowers grow where they are not wanted. Wildflowers that spread quickly in lawns, gardens, and similar places are sometimes called weeds. Many people consider the dandelion a weed because it spreads uninvited across carefully tended lawns. However, a weed to one person may be a beautiful wildflower to another.

COMMON SUNFLOWER

(HELIANTHUS ANNUUS)

The common sunflower grows on a tall, hairy stem. Each stem splits into branches that grow several bright yellow flowers with 17 to 40 petals. The flower's petals surround a dark, reddish-brown flower head. Each flower is about 3 to 5 inches (8 to 13 cm) wide. The sunflower's head moves to face the sun. Its toothed leaves are broad and either egg or heart shaped. Sunflowers produce edible seeds that are also used to make cooking oil.

HOW TO SPOT

Size: 2 to 13 feet (0.6 to 4 m) tall
North American Range: Alaska, Canada, and the United States, south to Costa Rica
Habitat: Prairies, roadsides, and fields
Bloom Period: June to November

FUN FACT

The Hopi people have traditionally used sunflowers to create dyes for use in crafting baskets and dying wool and cotton.

NEW ENGLAND ASTER

(SYMPHYOTRICHUM NOVAE-ANGLIAE)

The New England aster is one of the largest flowers in the aster family. Its flower heads measure more than 1 inch (2.5 cm) wide. The flowers have 35 to 45 purplish-blue, ray-shaped petals around a yellow center. They grow on stalks covered in short white hairs. The plant's hairy, toothless leaves are long and lance shaped. The New England aster blooms late, allowing it to supply nectar for migrating butterflies.

FUN FACT

The New England aster is also called the Michaelmas daisy because the flowers are often still in bloom for the feast of Saint Michael, called Michaelmas, at the end of September.

HOW TO SPOT

Size: 3 to 7 feet (0.9 to 2.1 m) tall

North American Range: Throughout most of Canada and the United States

Habitat: Meadows, fields, swamps, roadsides, and wet, heavily wooded areas

Bloom Period: August to October

OXEYE DAISY

(LEUCANTHEMUM VULGARE)

The oxeye daisy is easily spotted by its white ray-like petals around a bright yellow center. Each flower has between 15 and 25 petals. The flowers grow to be about 2 to 3 inches (5 to 8 cm) wide. The oxeye daisy's leaves are long and lobed. Larger leaves are near the stem's bottom, while smaller leaves grow farther up the stem.

FUN FACT

The word *daisy* comes from the phrase "day's eye" because these flowers open with the sun and close at night.

HOW TO SPOT

Size: 8 to 31 inches (20 to 79 cm) tall

North American Range: Throughout most of Canada and the United States

Habitat: Meadows, pastures, fields, and roadsides

Bloom Period: May to October

PURPLE CONEFLOWER

(ECHINACEA PURPUREA)

The purple coneflower has 15 to 20 drooping, magenta petals around a brown central cone-shaped disk. Each flower grows up to 5 inches (13 cm) wide and sits on a stiff, sometimes hairy stem. The plant's lance-shaped leaves have jagged edges and may or may not be hairy. Leaves mainly grow alternately on the stem but can be opposite. The flower's scientific name is from the Greek word *echinos*, which means "hedgehog," after its spiny center.

HOW TO SPOT

Size: 1 to 5 feet (0.3 to 1.5 m) tall

North American Range: Ontario in Canada, central and eastern United States

Habitat: Open woodlands, thickets, prairies, and dry forest edges

Bloom Period: June to October

FUN FACT

The purple coneflower's seed heads provide food for birds through the winter months.

SHOWY GOLDENROD

(SOLIDAGO SPECIOSA)

Showy goldenrod blooms have many small, bright yellow flowers. The flowers grow in dense clusters on a pyramid-shaped column that stands straight or curves outward. Each cluster can be up to 12 inches (30 cm) long. The showy goldenrod has a sturdy stem with oval leaves that grow alternately on the stem. The upper leaves are smaller than the lower leaves. Most of the showy goldenrod's leaves have smooth edges.

HOW TO SPOT

Size: 2 to 7 feet (0.6 to 2.1 m) tall

North American Range: Manitoba and Ontario in Canada, central and eastern United States (except Florida)

Habitat: Woodlands, prairies, and thickets

Bloom Period: August to October

SMOOTH BLUE ASTER

(SYMPHYOTRICHUM LAEVE)

The smooth blue aster is also known as the bluebird smooth aster. It can be recognized by its many lavender-blue, ray-like petals. The flower's petals surround a yellow center, forming a flower head that is about 1 inch (2.5 cm) wide. The flowers grow in branched clusters. The leaves are smooth, giving the plant its name. The long, oval-shaped leaves are thick and have a slightly jagged edge.

HOW TO SPOT

Size: 2 to 4 feet (0.6 to 1.2 m) tall

North American Range: Throughout most of Canada and the United States

Habitat: Open woodlands, fields, and rocky areas

Bloom Period: August to October

SWEET GOLDENROD

(SOLIDAGO ODORA)

The sweet goldenrod is known for its anise or licorice scent. The plant grows with clusters of small golden-yellow flowers along one side of a branch-like stem. Tiny flower heads measure about 0.13 inches (3 mm) wide. The flowers mature into small, tufted fruit. Narrow, lance-shaped leaves have smooth edges. The Cherokee used sweet goldenrod in traditional medicines. In colonial America, people brewed tea made from sweet goldenrod.

HOW TO SPOT

Size: 2 to 3 feet (0.6 to 0.9 m) tall

North American Range: Texas, Missouri, Ohio, and the East Coast of the United States from Vermont to Florida

Habitat: Fields and open woods

Bloom Period: July to September

COMMON JEWELWEED

(IMPATIENS CAPENSIS)

Common jewelweed is also called spotted touch-me-not or orange jewelweed. Its bright orange trumpet-shaped flowers have red or brown spots and hang like little jewels. Each flower is about 1 inch (2.5 cm) long. Long oval leaves with toothed edges grow alternately on the stem. When the seed pods are lightly touched, they pop open and scatter seeds. The plant's juice and leaves can soothe bug bites or poison ivy irritation.

HOW TO SPOT

Size: 2 to 5 feet (0.6 to 1.5 m) tall

North American Range: Alaska, most of Canada, Colorado through the East Coast of the United States

Habitat: Woodlands, wetlands, and other shady, damp areas

Bloom Period: July to October

FUN FACT

Sap from the common jewelweed prevents the growth of fungi and can be used to treat athlete's foot.

PALE TOUCH-ME-NOT

(IMPATIENS PALLIDA)

Pale touch-me-not is also called yellow or pale jewelweed. It has light yellow flowers that are funnel shaped and sometimes have reddish spots. Flowers grow 1 to 1.5 inches (2.5 to 4 cm) long. The plant's smooth, oval leaves are wide with toothed edges and alternate on heavily branched stems. Mature plants produce a small oval-shaped fruit that sprays seeds when dried or touched. Indigenous people made salves from the plant to treat skin conditions.

HOW TO SPOT

Size: 2 to 6 feet (0.6 to 1.8 m) tall

North American Range: Ontario and eastern Canada, south to Oklahoma and Alabama in the United States

Habitat: Meadows, stream banks, and moist, shady woodland edges

Bloom Period: July to September

MUSTARD FAMILY

BLACK MUSTARD *(BRASSICA NIGRA)*

Black mustard grows in clusters of yellow, four-petaled flowers from branched stems. The flowers measure about 0.4 inches (1 cm) wide. The plant's lower leaves each have one large lobe and four smaller lobes, while upper leaves are toothed and lance shaped. The plant's seeds are ground and used as a spice or to make mustard. In the past, black mustard leaves were used to treat colds and bronchitis.

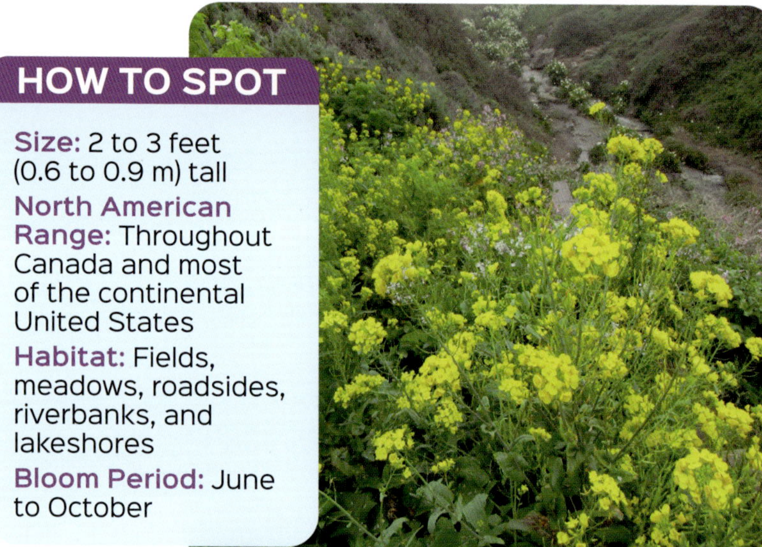

HOW TO SPOT

Size: 2 to 3 feet (0.6 to 0.9 m) tall

North American Range: Throughout Canada and most of the continental United States

Habitat: Fields, meadows, roadsides, riverbanks, and lakeshores

Bloom Period: June to October

FUN FACT

The ancient Egyptians put mustard seeds in the tombs of the pharaohs so they could have them in the afterlife.

VIRGINIA PEPPERWEED

(LEPIDIUM VIRGINICUM)

Virginia pepperweed, also called poorman's pepperwort, produces clusters of small white flowers. Each flower has four petals and is about 0.13 inches (3 mm) wide. The plant's long, toothed leaves grow alternately on the stem. The leaves are high in protein, vitamin A, and vitamin C and can be eaten raw or cooked. The plant forms a dry, rounded pod filled with seeds that can be used like black pepper.

HOW TO SPOT

Size: 6 to 24 inches (15 to 61 cm) tall
North American Range: Throughout most of North America
Habitat: Roadsides and other disturbed areas
Bloom Period: June to November

JAPANESE HONEYSUCKLE

(LONICERA JAPONICA)

Japanese honeysuckle is a fast-growing vine with fragrant flowers that bloom in late spring to summer. The white or yellow tube-shaped flowers are about 1.5 inches (4 cm) long and have a sweet scent. Flowers produce a nectar that can be sucked from each flower's base. The plant also produces small black berries that are not edible. Hairy, egg-shaped leaves are long and have smooth edges. The plant is considered an invasive species in North America.

HOW TO SPOT

Size: Up to 30 feet (9 m) long

North American Range: Central and eastern United States

Habitat: Thickets, woodlands, open areas, and roadsides

Bloom Period: April to July, sometimes through September

TRUMPET HONEYSUCKLE

(LONICERA SEMPERVIRENS)

Trumpet honeysuckle is a climbing vine with long, twisting stems and deep green or blue oval leaves that grow opposite on the stem. Its bright trumpet-shaped flowers are red on the outside and yellow or orange on the inside. Flowers are about 2 inches (5 cm) long and grow in whorled clusters at the top of stems. The plant produces a small red berry-like fruit.

HOW TO SPOT

Size: 10 to 15 feet (3 to 4.6 m) long

North American Range: Ontario and Quebec in Canada, central and eastern United States

Habitat: Woodlands, thickets, and gardens

Bloom Period: April to August

CARNATION FAMILY

BLADDER CAMPION

(SILENE VULGARIS)

Bladder campion, also called maidenstears, is native to Europe, Asia, and Northern Africa. The flowers are about 0.5 inches (1.3 cm) wide with five white petals and a pinkish-green calyx. A calyx is a whorl of sepals that form a cup around the flower's base. The flower has tall, thin stems with oval, tapered leaves that grow opposite on stems. The plant's shoots and leaves are edible.

HOW TO SPOT

Size: Up to 3 feet (0.9 m) tall

North American Range: Most of North America

Habitat: Fields and roadsides

Bloom Period: June to August

CLIMATE CHANGE

Climate change is affecting the balance of North American ecosystems and the wildflowers that grow in them. Early snowmelt, forest fires, changing temperatures and rainfall amounts, and extreme weather events can affect where wildflowers grow and survive. As a result, some wildflowers are beginning to grow in different areas.

CARDINAL CATCHFLY

(SILENE LACINIATA)

Cardinal catchfly is a bright red wildflower. Its five petals are long and deeply cut. The flower looks similar to star-like fireworks. This flower blooms in the summer and attracts hummingbirds, which help spread its pollen. It grows on a slender stem that may lean against other stems for support. Its long, narrow leaves have sticky hairs and grow opposite on the stem.

HOW TO SPOT

Size: 1 to 2.5 feet (0.3 to 0.8 m) tall

North American Range: California to Texas and south to Mexico

Habitat: Sunny meadows, hillsides, and open forests

Bloom Period: May to August

CARNATION FAMILY

COMMON CHICKWEED

(STELLARIA MEDIA)

Common chickweed has star-shaped flowers that are about 0.25 inches (6 mm) wide. Each flower has five petals that look like ten because they are split in half. The plant's broad, oval leaves have smooth edges that taper to a pointed tip and grow opposite on the stem. The plant spreads quickly along the ground. Birds love to eat chickweed, which is how it got its name. It is also an important food for insects.

HOW TO SPOT

Size: 3 to 8 inches (8 to 20 cm) tall

North American Range: Throughout North America

Habitat: Lawns, fields, and disturbed areas

Bloom Period: February to December

CORNCOCKLE *(AGROSTEMMA GITHAGO)*

Corncockle is a small wildflower with five bright purplish-pink petals and a white center. Each flower grows about 1 inch (2.5 cm) wide. It grows in farm fields, especially among crops such as wheat. It has a slender, hairy green stem and opposing narrow leaves. Corncockle blooms in the summer and attracts bees and butterflies. However, the plant is poisonous to many other animals and humans if eaten.

HOW TO SPOT

Size: 1 to 3 feet (0.3 to 0.9 m) tall

North American Range: Alaska, Saskatchewan to New Brunswick in Canada, throughout most of the continental United States (except Arizona, Utah, and Nevada)

Habitat: Fields, meadows, and roadsides

Bloom Period: May to July

DEPTFORD PINK *(DIANTHUS ARMERIA)*

Deptford pink, also called mountain pink, is a small, deep pink wildflower with tiny white spots around its center. The flower has five slightly jagged petals, making it look like a little star. The plant's thin, erect leaves grow in opposite pairs on the stem. Plants may have one or more stems. A single flower approximately 1 inch (2.5 cm) wide blooms on a stem or in small clusters along a branching stem.

HOW TO SPOT

Size: 8 to 24 inches (20 to 61 cm) tall

North American Range: Most of Canada and the continental United States

Habitat: Fields, pastures, roadsides, and woodland edges

Bloom Period: June to August

MAIDEN PINK *(DIANTHUS DELTOIDES)*

Maiden pink, also called lady's cushion, is a small, bright pink wildflower about 0.4 inches (1 cm) wide. It has five petals with tiny dark spots and toothed edges. A dark band near the base of each petal forms a ring around the flower's center. The plant's thin, narrow leaves taper to a pointed tip and grow in opposite pairs. Maiden pink produces many flowers, making it a beautiful ground cover plant.

HOW TO SPOT

Size: 4 to 16 inches (10 to 41 cm) tall

North American Range: Canada and most of the northern half of the United States

Habitat: Meadows, roadsides, fields, and trail edges

Bloom Period: June to August

FUN FACT

Some bakers use maiden pink flowers dipped in sugar to decorate cakes.

STARRY CAMPION *(SILENE STELLATA)*

Starry campion is also called widow's frill and whorled catchfly. It has white flowers that look like tiny stars. Each flower has five petals with deep cuts that look like fringe. The flowers are surrounded by bell-shaped sepals and are about 0.75 inches (2 cm) wide. The plant's smooth, tapered leaves grow in whorls on the stem, with some leaves growing in opposite pairs.

HOW TO SPOT

Size: 2 to 3 feet (0.6 to 0.9 m) tall

North American Range: Central and eastern United States (except Florida)

Habitat: Open woods, thickets, meadows, and prairies

Bloom Period: June to September

SWEET SAND-VERBENA

(ABRONIA FRAGRANS)

Sweet sand-verbena is also called fragrant verbena or snowball sand verbena. The plant forms round clusters of tiny, white, pale pink, green, or lavender funnel-shaped flowers that look like snowballs. Flower clusters grow to about 2 inches (5 cm) wide. The flowers open in the late afternoon and close in the morning. The plant has upright stems that are hairy and sticky with bright, hairy leaves. This plant tolerates hot, dry weather.

HOW TO SPOT

Size: 8 to 40 inches (20 to 102 cm) tall

North American Range: Montana and North Dakota south to Chihuahua and Coahuila in Mexico

Habitat: Sandy plains, pastures, savannas, and woodland edges

Bloom Period: April to September

GOURD FAMILY

ONE-SEEDED BUR CUCUMBER

(SICYOS ANGULATUS)

The one-seeded bur cucumber is also called the star cucumber. The white, star-shaped blooms form on a vine with hairy stems. The vines grow across the ground or cling to nearby structures using tendrils. The white flowers have five petals and are about 0.5 inches (1.3 cm) wide. The leaves are long and wide with three to five lobes. The plant produces a cucumber-like fruit that is covered with bristles. The fruit is not edible.

FUN FACT

The prickly fruit from the one-seeded bur cucumber sticks to the fur of animals. The animals help distribute the plant's seeds.

HOW TO SPOT

Size: 5 to 20 feet (1.5 to 6 m) long

North American Range: Ontario and Quebec in Canada, central and eastern United States

Habitat: Stream banks, thickets, roadsides, and woodland edges

Bloom Period: July to September

WILD CUCUMBER

(ECHINOCYSTIS LOBATA)

Wild cucumber is a fast-growing vine that climbs trees, fences, and bushes. It has big leaves with three to seven pointed, triangular lobes. Its small, white, star-shaped flowers have six petals, are about 0.5 inches (1.3 cm) wide, and smell sweet. The plant grows spiky green fruit pods that look like tiny cucumbers. The fruits are not edible. When the pods mature and dry, they pop open and spread seeds.

HOW TO SPOT

Size: Up to 30 feet (9 m) long

North American Range: Throughout Canada and the United States

Habitat: Moist woodlands and stream banks

Bloom Period: June to October

Wild cucumber fruit pods

COMMON MORNING GLORY

(IPOMOEA PURPUREA)

The common morning glory has large, funnel-shaped flowers. Flowers are usually purple but may also be blue, pink, or white and range from 1 to 3 inches (2.5 to 8 cm) wide. The flowers grow on a vine with large, alternate, heart-shaped leaves. The vine climbs or spreads across the ground. The flowers open in the morning. The common morning glory is native to Mexico and Central America.

HOW TO SPOT

Size: 3 to 10 feet (0.9 to 3 m) long

North American Range: Throughout North America

Habitat: Fields, roadsides, and disturbed areas

Bloom Period: July to October

SMALL WHITE MORNING GLORY

(IPOMOEA LACUNOSA)

The small white morning glory grows on a vine that climbs or spreads across the ground. The funnel-shaped flowers are usually white but may also be light purple or pink. The flowers have five petals and are about 0.75 inches (2 cm) wide. The plant's vines can be hairy with alternating leaves. Larger leaves are heart shaped, while smaller leaves are egg shaped. Each stalk supports one to three flowers.

HOW TO SPOT

Size: 3 to 7 feet (0.9 to 2.1 m) long

North American Range: Central to eastern United States

Habitat: Fields, roadsides, and other disturbed areas

Bloom Period: July to October

BIRD'S-FOOT TREFOIL

(LOTUS CORNICULATUS)

Bird's-foot trefoil is also known as "eggs and bacon." It grows low to the ground and produces 0.5-inch (1.3-cm) wide bright yellow, pea-shaped flowers with three petals. The yellow flowers grow in clusters and can become orange or red as they age. The plant is named for its seed pods, which look like a bird's foot. Alternate leaves have five leaflets, with three near the tip of the leaf stalk and two near its base.

HOW TO SPOT

Size: 3 to 12 inches (8 to 30 cm) tall
North American Range: Throughout most of Canada and the United States
Habitat: Fields and roadsides
Bloom Period: May to September

COW VETCH *(VICIA CRACCA)*

Cow vetch is a climbing plant with dangling, pea-like flowers that are about 0.5 inches (1.3 cm) long. The reddish-lavender to purplish-blue flowers bloom on one side of a stalk in clusters of 10 to 50. Its compound leaves have 19 to 29 leaflets with smooth edges and an oval shape. The cow vetch is commonly grazed by cattle. Seeds of some vetch species, including cow vetch, contain cyanide. This is a poisonous chemical found naturally in some plants.

HOW TO SPOT

Size: 1 to 3 feet (0.3 to 0.9 m) tall

North American Range: Canada and northern United States

Habitat: Fields and roadsides

Bloom Period: May to July

PURPLE PRAIRIE CLOVER

(DALEA PURPUREA)

The purple prairie clover has small, purple flowers with five petals that bloom closely together along a cone-shaped flower head. The tiny flowers have yellow-tipped stamen. The flower head is 0.5 to 2.5 inches (1.3 to 6.4 cm) long. Small, compound leaves with three to seven leaflets are densely packed in an alternate pattern around the plant's lower stem. It is a nutritious source of food for wildlife.

HOW TO SPOT

Size: 1 to 3 feet (0.3 to 0.9 m) tall

North American Range: British Columbia to Manitoba in Canada, south to Alabama and west to Arizona in the United States

Habitat: Prairies and dry hillsides

Bloom Period: May to August

RED CLOVER *(TRIFOLIUM PRATENSE)*

Red clover is a member of the pea family. Usually its flowers are pinkish red, but sometimes they can be red or white. The flowers are 0.5 to 0.75 inches (1.3 to 2 cm) wide and grow in round or egg-shaped clusters. The flowers smell like honey. The compound leaves have three oval leaflets with smooth edges. Bumblebees are the most common pollinators for this wildflower species.

HOW TO SPOT

Size: 1 to 3 feet (0.3 to 0.9 m) tall

North American Range: Most of Canada and the United States

Habitat: Fields, lawns, meadows, pastures, and roadsides

Bloom Period: June to August

WHITE CLOVER *(TRIFOLIUM REPENS)*

White clover has a round flower head with many tiny white pea-shaped flowers. The flower heads are about 0.5 inches (1.3 cm) wide and grow on a slim, smooth stalk that rises about 3 inches (8 cm) above a horizontal stem on the ground. The flower's white petals turn pink as they mature. The compound leaves have three broad, oval leaflets with finely toothed edges that grow in an alternate pattern on the stem.

HOW TO SPOT

Size: 4 to 24 inches (10 to 61 cm) tall

North American Range: Most of Canada and the United States

Habitat: Fields, roadsides, and lawns

Bloom Period: April to September

FUN FACT

White clover that produces four leaflets instead of three is considered good luck according to Irish legend.

WHITE WILD INDIGO *(BAPTISIA ALBA)*

The white wild indigo grows in long spikes of pea-shaped white flowers. The flowers are about 1 inch (2.5 cm) long and grow on 6-to-9-inch (15-to-23-cm) spikes. The upper petal has a purple mark near its base. The plant's branching stems have alternating compound leaves. Each leaf has three leaflets with smooth edges. As the plant matures, the flowers die and seed pods grow in their place. Butterfly larvae commonly use the white wild indigo plant as food.

HOW TO SPOT

Size: 2 to 5 feet (0.6 to 1.5 m) tall

North American Range: Central and eastern United States

Habitat: Prairies, open woodlands, roadsides, and near marshes and lakes

Bloom Period: May to July

ROCKY MOUNTAIN IRIS

(IRIS MISSOURIENSIS)

The Rocky Mountain iris produces large flowers that range in color from pale to dark purple, often with white or yellow markings. One to four flowers grow on each stem, with each flower being 2 to 3 inches (5 to 8 cm) long. The plant's leaves are sword shaped and greenish gray in color. Its fibers are very strong and are sometimes used to make ropes, strings, and fishing nets.

HOW TO SPOT

Size: 1 to 2 feet (0.3 to 0.6 m) tall

North American Range: Western and central North America

Habitat: Marshy meadows and along riverbanks

Bloom Period: May to July

SOUTHERN BLUE FLAG

(IRIS VIRGINICA)

The Southern blue flag, also called the Virginia blue flag, has small blue or purple flowers with a bright yellow base. The flowers are 1.5 inches (4 cm) wide and have three sepals that curve upward and three sepals that curve down. Long, sword-shaped leaves are primarily found near the plant's base. Caterpillars and other insects feed on the plant. The Cherokee people have long used the roots to treat skin ailments and the leaves to make baskets.

HOW TO SPOT

Size: 1 to 3 feet (0.3 to 0.9 m) tall

North American Range: Ontario to Quebec in Canada, central and eastern United States

Habitat: Marshes, wetlands, and along lakes, ponds, and streams

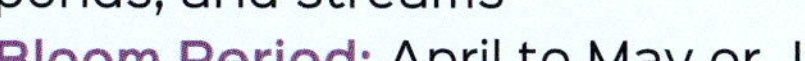

Bloom Period: April to May or June

AMERICAN WILD MINT

(MENTHA CANADENSIS)

American wild mint, also known as Canadian mint, is a common, sweet-smelling herb. The plant has small, tube-shaped flowers that can be pink, purple, or violet and grow in bunches. Each flower is about 0.2 to 0.3 inches (0.5 to 0.8 cm) long. The plant has large, hairy, egg-shaped leaves with jagged edges. They grow in opposite pairs on the stem. The leaves can be used to add mint flavor to drinks, jellies, and sauces.

HOW TO SPOT

Size: 4 to 18 inches (10 to 46 cm) tall

North American Range: Alaska, throughout most of Canada, the United States, and Mexico

Habitat: Wet areas alongside lakes and rivers

Bloom Period: July to August

LEAF MARGINS

The edge of a leaf is called its margin. Some leaves have smooth margins. Some are toothed, giving the margin a jagged look. Lobed leaves have large divisions. Some leaf margins are rounded or wavy. Other margins have many small cuts, making them appear fringed.

CATNIP *(NEPETA CATARIA)*

Catnip, also known as catmint, usually grows in clumps with tall, erect stems topped with clustered white to pale lavender flowers with purple spots. The tube-shaped flowers are 0.4 to 0.5 inches (1 to 1.3 cm) long. The heart-shaped or oval leaves have rounded teeth and are covered in fuzzy hairs. Many cats like to rub against the plant's leaves. The plant has been used in medicine to reduce anxiety and improve mood.

FUN FACT

Catnip can make cats relaxed or excited and playful. Not all cats are affected by catnip, only those with a specific gene.

HOW TO SPOT

Size: 1 to 3 feet (0.3 to 0.9 m) tall

North American Range: Alaska, Canada, and most of the continental United States

Habitat: Pastures, barnyards, and roadsides

Bloom Period: June to September

HOARY VERVAIN *(VERBENA STRICTA)*

Hoary vervain grows in clumps and is named after the stiff hairs on its stem and leaves. The stem branches into several flowering spikes, producing small lavender to blue flowers approximately 0.5 inches (1.3 cm) wide that bloom about halfway down each spike. The flowers have five petals that form a tube shape. The plant's opposite, egg-shaped leaves have jagged edges and are covered in white hairs.

HOW TO SPOT

Size: 1 to 4 feet (0.3 to 1.2 m) tall

North American Range: Ontario and Quebec in Canada, most of the continental United States

Habitat: Meadows, prairies, and fields

Bloom Period: July to September

NARROWLEAF MOUNTAIN MINT

(PYCNANTHEMUM TENUIFOLIUM)

The narrowleaf mountain mint is a sweet-smelling herb. All parts of the plant give off a minty scent when crushed. The plant produces dense clusters of small, whitish flowers with purple spots and narrow, needle-like leaves. People have used narrowleaf mountain mint to flavor herbal teas. Bees and butterflies feed on the flower's nectar, while deer eat its leaves. Birds, small mammals, and other animals eat seeds from the plant.

HOW TO SPOT

Size: 2 to 3 feet (0.6 to 0.9 m) tall

North American Range: Ontario and Quebec in Canada, central and eastern United States

Habitat: Dry prairies, fields, open rocky woodlands, and roadsides

Bloom Period: July to September

MINT FAMILY

PURPLE DEAD NETTLE

(LAMIUM PURPUREUM)

Purple dead nettle is native to Europe and Asia. Its reddish square stem produces dense clusters of reddish-purple flowers that attract bees. The plant's hairy, heart-shaped leaves have wavy purple edges. The leaves contain iron, vitamins, and fiber and are sometimes used in salads and sauces.

HOW TO SPOT

Size: Up to 2 feet (0.6 m) tall
North American Range: Throughout North America
Habitat: Roadsides, untended areas, and other disturbed ground
Bloom Period: Year-round

PURPLE GIANT HYSSOP

(AGASTACHE SCROPHULARIIFOLIA)

The purple giant hyssop is a tall herb with sweet-smelling flowers that range in color from pale purple to a purplish red. The flowers bloom on a densely packed spike that measures 1 to 6 inches (2.5 to 15 cm) long. The purple giant hyssop has a square stem with short hairs. Its oval, opposite leaves have jagged edges and a whitish underside. This plant is a key source of nectar for butterflies.

HOW TO SPOT

Size: 2 to 5 feet (0.6 to 1.5 m) tall

North American Range: Ontario in Canada, central and eastern United States

Habitat: Woodlands, thickets, and wet areas

Bloom Period: July to September

ROSE MOCK VERVAIN

(GLANDULARIA CANADENSIS)

Rose mock vervain, also known as sweet william or rose vervain, is an herb with dense, round clusters of sweet-smelling pinkish-lavender or white flowers. The flowers have five petals and are about 0.5 to 0.75 inches (1.3 to 2 cm) wide. The plant has a hairy stem that can grow along the ground or upright. Its lobed, oval-shaped leaves grow opposite each other on the stem.

HOW TO SPOT

Size: 6 to 18 inches (15 to 46 cm) tall

North American Range: Central and eastern United States

Habitat: Prairies, pastures, fields, open woodlands, roadsides, and rocky areas

Bloom Period: April to October

SPOTTED BEEBALM

(MONARDA PUNCTATA)

The spotted beebalm is also known as horsemint. Its flowers are whitish yellow with purple spots and grow 3 to 6 inches (8 to 15 cm) long. Large, leafy-looking bracts grow underneath the flower's petals. The bracts range in color from pink to lavender or purple. The plant's pointed leaves have lightly jagged edges and grow in opposite pairs on the stem. The plant contains thymol, which is used to treat upset stomachs and colds.

HOW TO SPOT

Size: 0.5 to 3 feet (0.2 to 0.9 m) tall

North American Range: Central and eastern United States, northeastern Mexico

Habitat: Dry, sandy areas

Bloom Period: June to August

WILD BASIL *(CLINOPODIUM VULGARE)*

Wild basil, also known as field basil, is a common herb. It has a square, hairy stem topped with dense, round clusters of trumpet-shaped flowers. These flowers, which are about 0.5 inches (1.3 cm) long, can be rose pink, lavender, or white. Underneath the flowers, hairy bracts have a woolly appearance. Hairy, egg-shaped leaves have mostly smooth edges and grow in opposite pairs on the stem.

HOW TO SPOT

Size: 8 to 20 inches (20 to 51 cm) tall

North American Range: British Columbia and Ontario to Nova Scotia in Canada, northeastern, southwestern, and northwestern United States

Habitat: Pastures, thickets, and roadsides

Bloom Period: June to September

WILD BERGAMOT

(MONARDA FISTULOSA)

Wild bergamot has a square, hollow stem with pink or purple tube-shaped flowers. The flowers grow in clusters 1 to 2 inches (2.5 to 5 cm) wide around a honeycomb-like sphere. The plant's long, tapered leaves have jagged edges and grow in opposite pairs on the stem. Leaves have a hairy underside and a smooth or hairy surface. Wild bergamot's sweet-smelling leaves are often used in mint and herbal teas.

HOW TO SPOT

Size: 2 to 4 feet (0.6 to 1.2 m) tall

North American Range: Canada, the United States, northeastern Mexico

Habitat: Fields, thickets, pastures, and roadsides

Bloom Period: June to September

CANADA LILY *(LILIUM CANADENSE)*

The Canada lily is large and showy, with bell-shaped flowers that hang like little lanterns from tall, thin stems. Flowers are yellow, orange, or red with brown spots and grow 2 to 3 inches (5 to 8 cm) wide. Six dusty brown stamens hang from the flower's center. Each plant has four to ten narrow, whorled, spear-shaped leaves with little prickles underneath. The Algonquin people used the plant to treat stomach illnesses.

HOW TO SPOT

Size: Up to 6 feet (1.8 m) tall

North American Range: Eastern Canada and eastern United States

Habitat: Wet meadows, woodland borders, riverbanks, and stream banks

Bloom Period: June to August

FUN FACT

Lilies are associated with Hera, who is the goddess of women, marriage, family, and childbirth in Greek mythology.

CHECKER LILY *(FRITILLARIA AFFINIS)*

The checker lily is also called the chocolate lily. It has tall, slender green stems with narrow, lance-shaped leaves and hanging, bell-shaped flowers. The petals are usually dark brownish purple with a mottled pattern, though some may be yellow or purple with yellowish-green mottling. Flowers grow up to 1.5 inches (4 cm) wide. Leaves grow in a whorl pattern around the stem. The plant grows from an underground bulb, which the Coast and Interior Salish people used for food.

HOW TO SPOT

Size: 8 to 20 inches (20 to 51 cm)

North American Range: Western Canada and western United States

Habitat: Moist meadows and grassy areas, coastal areas, and open woodlands

Bloom Period: April to July

GUNNISON'S MARIPOSA LILY

(CALOCHORTUS GUNNISONII)

Gunnison's mariposa lily has tall, thin stems with grass-like leaves and large, cup-shaped flowers. The flower has three petals that are usually white or pale purple and look similar to butterfly wings. The petals surround a yellow to dark purple fringed center. The plant's long, thin leaves alternate on the stem and wither when its flowers bloom. The wildflower was named after Captain J. W. Gunnison, who died while leading an expedition to Utah in 1853.

HOW TO SPOT

Size: 6 to 18 inches (15 to 46 cm) tall

North American Range: Central western United States, from Montana to Arizona and New Mexico

Habitat: Mountain meadows, open woodlands, and prairies

Bloom Period: May to July

WOOD LILY *(LILIUM PHILADELPHICUM)*

The wood lily is a bright orange or red funnel-shaped flower with dark spots. Each stem usually supports one to three flowers, though there may be up to five. Flowers are 2 to 2.5 inches (5 to 6.4 cm) wide and have six petal-like tepals. Narrow, lance-shaped leaves with smooth edges grow in whorls on the stem. The plant grows from a bulb underground. Wood lilies attract pollinators, especially large swallowtail butterflies. The wood lily is becoming more rare.

HOW TO SPOT

Size: 12 to 28 inches (30 to 71 cm) tall

North American Range: Canada, central and eastern United States

Habitat: Open woodlands, prairies, thickets, and roadsides

Bloom Period: June to August

FRAGRANT WATER-LILY

(NYMPHAEA ODORATA)

The fragrant water-lily, or American white water-lily, has large, round leaves called lily pads that float on the water. Its bright white flowers have yellow centers and a sweet smell. The flowers are 3 to 6 inches (8 to 15 cm) wide and have 20 to 30 petals. They open in the morning and close at night. The blooms last only a few days and then sink into the water, where the fruit matures.

HOW TO SPOT

Size: 2 to 4 feet (0.6 to 1.2 m) tall

North American Range: Most of Canada, the United States, Mexico, south to Nicaragua

Habitat: Freshwater shallow ponds, lakes, and slow-moving rivers

Bloom Period: July to October

FUN FACT

French painter Claude Monet featured water lilies in many of his famous paintings.

YELLOW POND-LILY

(NUPHAR ADVENA)

The yellow pond-lily, also called spatterdock, grows in fresh bodies of water. Its bright yellow flowers stand above the water on thick stems. These flowers measure 1 to 2 inches (2.5 to 5 cm) wide and look like small cups. The large, heart-shaped leaves are called lily pads and float on or near the water's surface. The plant's roots grow in the muddy bottom.

HOW TO SPOT

Size: 7.2 to 24 inches (18 to 60 cm) tall

North American Range: Ontario south to northeast Mexico, east to the East Coast of the United States

Habitat: Freshwater ponds, lakes, and slow-moving rivers

Bloom Period: March to October

COMMON EVENING PRIMROSE

(OENOTHERA BIENNIS)

Common evening primrose has bright yellow, lemon-scented flowers. Each flower has four rounded petals and is 1 to 2 inches (2.5 to 5 cm) wide. The flowers bloom in the evening and stay open overnight before closing and withering by noon. The plant's sturdy stem is covered in soft hairs. Long, lance-shaped leaves with wavy or slightly jagged edges grow in an alternate pattern near the plant's base.

FUN FACT

The evening primrose uses a light-sensitive pigment called phytochrome to sense whether it is day or night.

HOW TO SPOT

Size: 2 to 5 feet (0.6 to 1.5 m) tall
North American Range: Canada south to central Mexico
Habitat: Fields and roadsides
Bloom Period: June to September

CUTLEAF EVENING PRIMROSE

(OENOTHERA LACINIATA)

The cutleaf evening primrose has pale yellow, cup-shaped flowers that bloom in the evening and close the next day. Each flower is approximately 0.5 to 1.5 inches (1.3 to 4 cm) wide and has four heart-shaped petals and several yellow stamens in the center. The plant's leaves are sometimes hairy and have an oval shape with irregular toothed edges. Leaves grow in an alternate pattern near the plant's base.

HOW TO SPOT

Size: 6 to 30 inches (15 to 76 cm) tall

North American Range: Ontario in Canada, throughout the United States, Mexico south to Guatemala

Habitat: Fields and open spaces

Bloom Period: March to October

SHOWY EVENING PRIMROSE

(OENOTHERA SPECIOSA)

The showy evening primrose, also called pink ladies, is known for its delicate pink or white flowers. The large, cup-shaped flowers have four rounded petals and are about 2 to 3.5 inches (5 to 9 cm) wide. The petals have pink or red veins and fade to white near the base. The leaves are narrow and tapered. The showy evening primrose blooms in the evening and often stays open at night.

HOW TO SPOT

Size: 8 to 24 inches (20 to 61 cm) tall

North American Range: Central United States south to central Mexico

Habitat: Prairies, meadows, open woodlands, and roadsides

Bloom Period: May to July

TUFTED EVENING PRIMROSE

(OENOTHERA CAESPITOSA)

The tufted evening primrose has large white flowers that are 3 to 4 inches (8 to 10 cm) wide and last a single night before they fade to pink and wither. The blossoms, which include four heart-shaped petals, have a sweet smell. The flower sits on a rosette of lance-shaped leaves with wavy edges that grow near the plant's base.

HOW TO SPOT

Size: Up to 12 inches (30 cm) tall

North American Range: Central Canada, western and central United States

Habitat: Open woodlands, clearings, hillsides, canyons, and roadsides

Bloom Period: April to August

DRAGON'S MOUTH ORCHID

(ARETHUSA BULBOSA)

The dragon's mouth orchid produces one pink to magenta flower. The bloom, which is 1 to 3 inches (2.5 to 8 cm) long, resembles a mouth that has a whitish-pink lip with magenta spots and a yellow center. The flower has three oval sepals and two petals that form a hood over a lower lip. The plant has one long, grass-like leaf. People collect this orchid, so the plant's numbers in the wild are shrinking.

HOW TO SPOT

Size: 3 to 14 inches (8 to 35 cm) tall

North American Range: Alberta east to Newfoundland in Canada, northeast and north central United States

Habitat: Wet meadows, swamps, peat bogs, and lakeshores

Bloom Period: June to July

STRUCTURE OF AN ORCHID

Orchids have a unique structure made of four main parts. The orchid's flower has an outer layer of three sepals, which protect the flower bud. When the flower blooms, the sepals are often large and brightly colored. Inside the whorl of sepals are three inner petals. The bottom petal is usually large and showy and is called a lip. The lip may be colored, marked, or decorated to attract pollinators. A single column in the center of the orchid holds the plant's pollen.

DWARF RATTLESNAKE PLANTAIN *(GOODYERA REPENS)*

The dwarf rattlesnake plantain is also called the lesser rattlesnake plantain. The plant produces up to 36 small, white flowers that are approximately 0.13 inches (3 mm) wide. Each flower has a cupped lip and a curved hood over the petals and sepals. Its stem and sepals are covered with thin hairs. Most leaves grow near the plant's base and are oval or egg shaped. Some leaves have a green-and-white pattern.

HOW TO SPOT

Size: 1.2 to 10 inches (3 to 25 cm) tall

North American Range: Alaska, Canada, and parts of eastern, central, and southwestern United States

Habitat: Moist woodlands, meadows, forests, and floodplains

Bloom Period: July to September

LESSER PURPLE FRINGED ORCHID *(PLATANTHERA PSYCODES)*

The lesser purple fringed orchid has many small white, pink, or purple flowers that bloom along the tip of the stem. The flowers are 0.5 to 0.75 inches (1.3 to 2 cm) long and have a three-lobed lip and fringe that looks like a butterfly. Oval leaves with pointed tips and smooth edges grow alternately on the stem. The plant's Latin name is from the Greek goddess Psyche, who was represented by a butterfly.

HOW TO SPOT

Size: 1 to 3 feet (0.3 to 0.9 m) tall

North American Range: Eastern Canada, central and northeast United States

Habitat: Meadows, swamps, bogs, and along rivers and streams

Bloom Period: June to August

LILY-LEAVED TWAYBLADE

(LIPARIS LILIIFOLIA)

The lily-leaved twayblade is also called the mauve sleekwort. It produces 6 to 24 pale purple to brown flowers that have a wide, flat labellum, or lip. Each flower is approximately 0.6 inches (1.5 cm) long. The flower's long, thin petals and sepals droop away from the flower. Two oval, pointed, and glossy leaves grow near the plant's base.

HOW TO SPOT

Size: 3 to 10 inches (8 to 25 cm) tall

North American Range: Ontario in Canada, central and eastern United States

Habitat: Woodlands, thickets, and old-growth forests, especially among pine trees

Bloom Period: June to July

PINK LADY'S SLIPPER

(CYPRIPEDIUM ACAULE)

The pink lady's slipper is named for its resemblance to a shoe. The flower has an inflated bright pink labellum, or lip, with dark pink areas. Each flower is about 2.5 inches (6.4 cm) long. The flower's sweet smell attracts pollinating bumblebees, but the flower has no nectar. Each stalk usually produces a single flower. Two ribbed, oval leaves with silvery, hairy undersides grow at the base of the plant.

HOW TO SPOT

Size: 6 to 15 inches (15 to 38 cm) tall

North American Range: Central and eastern Canada, north central and eastern United States

Habitat: Dry to moist forests

Bloom Period: April to July

SHOWY LADY'S SLIPPER

(CYPRIPEDIUM REGINAE)

The showy lady's slipper is the tallest native North American orchid. Its hairy, leafy stem produces one to three large flowers. Each flower is approximately 1 to 2 inches (2.5 to 5 cm) long. The flower's white petals and sepals surround a deep pink labellum that looks like a round pouch. The plant's large, oval leaves are hairy with wavy edges. A plant can take more than 16 years to flower.

FUN FACT

The showy lady's slipper is the state flower of Minnesota.

HOW TO SPOT

Size: 8 to 39 inches (20 to 100 cm) tall

North American Range: Central and eastern Canada, north central and eastern United States

Habitat: Wetlands and moist woodlands

Bloom Period: May to August

WHITE FRINGED ORCHID

(PLATANTHERA BLEPHARIGLOTTIS)

The white fringed orchid is also known as the white fringed bog orchid. Its flowers have fluffy white petals with fringed edges that look like tiny wings. The plant thrives in wet areas. It has a tall stem that supports many blossoms. The plant's leaves are small and lance-shaped with smooth edges that grow in an alternate pattern on the stem.

HOW TO SPOT

Size: 3 to 43 inches (8 to 110 cm)

North American Range: Eastern Canada, north central, eastern, and southeast United States

Habitat: Moist woodlands, wet meadows, bogs, and marshes

Bloom Period: June to September

YELLOW LADY'S SLIPPER

(CYPRIPEDIUM PARVIFLORUM)

The yellow lady's slipper is also called the greater yellow lady's slipper and the moccasin flower. It looks like a tiny golden slipper. It has a bright yellow pouch-shaped bloom with curly brownish petals on the sides. This orchid adapts to the various environments throughout its range. Because of this there are three different varieties of this species. The flower sizes and the darkness of the sepals and petals differ between species. The oval-shaped leaves are arranged alternately on the stem.

HOW TO SPOT

Size: 8 to 28 inches (20 to 71 cm) tall

North American Range: Alaska, Canada, most of the United States

Habitat: Swamps, bogs, and woods

Bloom Period: April to August

ANNUAL PRICKLY POPPY

(ARGEMONE POLYANTHEMOS)

The annual prickly poppy is also called the crested prickly poppy. Each flower has four to six bright crinkly white petals with a yellow center. The flower grows about 3 inches (8 cm) wide. Leaves are lobed with prickly spines. Sharp, prickly leaves, stems, and fruits help protect the plant from animals. The plant also releases a poisonous yellow sap. The Shoshone, Paiute, Kawaiisu, and Comanche people used the poppy to treat sores, burns, and eye ailments.

HOW TO SPOT

Size: 3 to 4 feet (0.9 to 1.2 m) tall

North American Range: Central United States

Habitat: Plains, prairies, meadows, and roadsides

Bloom Period: April to July

CALIFORNIA POPPY

(ESCHSCHOLZIA CALIFORNICA)

The California poppy, also called the golden poppy, is the state flower of California. The flowers open in the sunlight and close at night or on cloudy days. The cup-shaped flower is usually bright orange but can be yellow or red. Each flower is 0.75 to 2.5 inches (2 to 6.4 cm) long. The plant's greenish-gray leaves are feathery. The California poppy can be poisonous to animals and humans if eaten.

FUN FACT

In the movie *The Wizard of Oz*, Dorothy falls asleep in a field of poppies.

HOW TO SPOT

Size: 8 to 24 inches (20 to 61 cm) tall

North American Range: Western and south central United States south to Mexico

Habitat: Open forests, meadows, plains, coastal dunes, and desert edges

Bloom Period: February to June and August to October

DUTCHMAN'S BREECHES

(DICENTRA CUCULLARIA)

Dutchman's breeches look like tiny white pants hanging upside down. Each flower is approximately 0.75 inches (2 cm) long with two pale yellow lobes that open at the flower's base. The flowers grow on a thin, curved stem. Compound leaves with three oval-shaped leaflets grow near the plant's base. Ants help spread the plant's seeds by carrying them underground. All parts of this wildflower are highly poisonous if eaten.

HOW TO SPOT

Size: 4 to 12 inches (10 to 30 cm) tall

North American Range: Eastern Canada; northwest, central, and eastern United States

Habitat: Forests

Bloom Period: April to May

GOLDEN SMOKE *(CORYDALIS AUREA)*

Golden smoke takes its name from its smoke-like scent. The plant's bright yellow tube-shaped flowers look like little trumpets. Flowers have two pairs of petals and are 0.5 to 0.75 inches (1.3 to 2 cm) long. Leaves are compound with multiple oval-shaped, pointed lobes that give them a feathery appearance. The wildflower commonly grows in areas where wildfires have cleared away other vegetation. The plant is poisonous to people and animals.

HOW TO SPOT

Size: 4 to 24 inches (10 to 61 cm) tall

North American Range: Alaska, Canada, western and central United States, northern Mexico

Habitat: Open prairies and woodlands, rocky hillsides

Bloom Period: February to September

GRANITE PRICKLY PHLOX

(LINANTHUS PUNGENS)

The granite prickly phlox, or granite gilia, has a funnel-shaped flower with five white petals around a yellow center. Flowers grow up to 1 inch (2.5 cm) long. Occasionally, they are pale yellow or pale pink. The flowers give off a strong scent. The phlox has several branching stems with thin, prickly leaves that have three to seven lobes. The plant can grow upright or along the ground.

HOW TO SPOT

Size: 4 to 32 inches (10 to 81 cm) tall

North American Range: Western Canada, western United States, western Mexico

Habitat: Woodlands, forests, grasslands, mountains, and alpine areas

Bloom Period: April to June

FUN FACT

The word *phlox* comes from the Greek word meaning "flame."

MOSS PINK *(PHLOX SUBULATA)*

Moss pink, also called moss phlox, grows close to the ground like a carpet. The creeping plant has flowers that grow in clusters. They are usually light pink or lavender and fade to white along the edges of five notched lobes. A circle of darker pink dots surrounds the flower's center. The flowers are about 0.75 inches (2 cm) wide. Long, needle-like leaves grow opposite or in whorls on the stem.

HOW TO SPOT

Size: 2 to 5 inches (5 to 13 cm) tall

North American Range: Central and eastern Canada, central and eastern United States

Habitat: Dry or sandy places, rocky slopes, and open woodlands

Bloom Period: April to May

NARROWLEAF MOUNTAIN-TRUMPET

(COLLOMIA LINEARIS)

The narrowleaf mountain-trumpet has a velvety stem that supports a cluster of about 20 small flowers. The flowers, which are approximately 0.4 inches (1 cm) wide, are pink, white, or lilac and have five small petals. Five sepals form a cup around the flower. The plant's narrow leaves are lance shaped and arranged alternately on the stem. The Gosiute people crushed the plant's leaves to make pastes and other treatments for bruises and injuries.

HOW TO SPOT

Size: 4 to 16 inches (10 to 41 cm) tall

North American Range: Alaska, Canada, western and northern United States

Habitat: Dry open woodlands, fields, and disturbed areas

Bloom Period: May to August

SKYROCKET *(IPOMOPSIS AGGREGATA)*

The skyrocket has distinct, tube-shaped bright red flowers ending in five lobes that spread out like a star. The flowers are also called skunk flowers for their unpleasant smell. This wildflower varies in size and color depending on where it grows. In higher elevations, the flowers can be pink or orange. The flowers are about 0.75 to 1.25 inches (2 to 3.2 cm) long. The leaves are fern-like and concentrated near the plant's base.

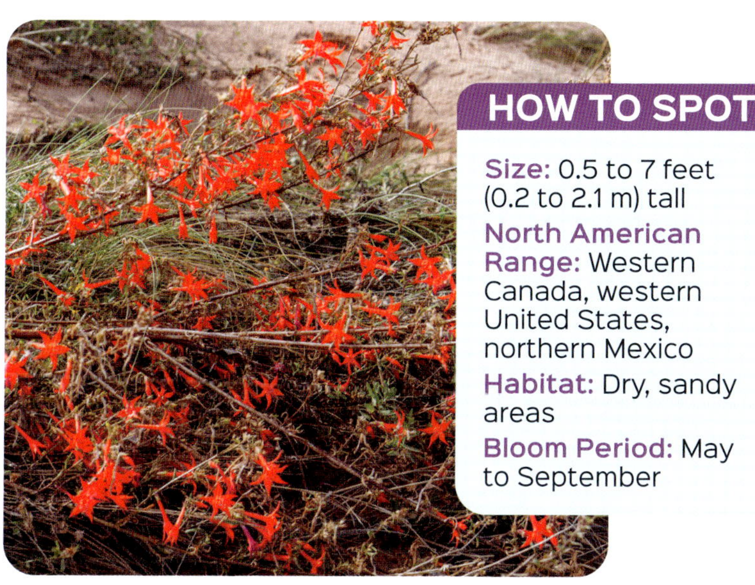

HOW TO SPOT

Size: 0.5 to 7 feet (0.2 to 2.1 m) tall

North American Range: Western Canada, western United States, northern Mexico

Habitat: Dry, sandy areas

Bloom Period: May to September

ROSE FAMILY

COMMON CINQUEFOIL

(POTENTILLA SIMPLEX)

The common cinquefoil has bright yellow flowers that grow on long, fuzzy stalks. Each flower is about 0.5 inches (1.3 cm) across, with five heart-shaped yellow petals around a yellow center. Its compound leaves are divided into five leaflets with jagged edges that are attached alternately on the stem. This plant spreads by creeping along the ground with long stems called runners, which help it grow new plants nearby.

HOW TO SPOT

Size: 8 to 12 inches (20 to 30 cm) tall

North American Range: Eastern Canada, central and eastern United States

Habitat: Open woodlands, prairies, and roadsides

Bloom Period: April to June

DWARF RED RASPBERRY

(RUBUS PUBESCENS)

Dwarf red raspberry is a small plant that thrives in cool, shady areas with moist soil. It has bright green leaves and hairy stems that spread by sending out runners along the ground. Its tiny white flowers are about 0.5 inches (1.3 cm) across and usually have five petals. The flowers turn into small, red raspberries. The plant's compound leaves have three leaflets and alternate on the stem. While many raspberry species have thorns, this one does not.

HOW TO SPOT

Side: 4 to 12 inches (10 to 30 cm) tall

North American Range: Alaska, Canada, northern United States

Habitat: Bogs, swamps, and other wetlands

Bloom Period: May to June

TALL CINQUEFOIL

(DRYMOCALLIS ARGUTA)

Tall cinquefoil, or prairie cinquefoil, has small, creamy white or pale yellow flowers. The flowers grow in clusters. Each flower has five petals with a yellow center and is about 0.5 to 0.75 inches (1.3 to 2 cm) across. Compound leaves have 7 to 11 leaflets and grow mainly near the plant's base. Leaflets are hairy and toothed. The plant's leaves provide food for deer and other mammals, and the flowers provide nectar for bees and butterflies.

HOW TO SPOT

Size: 1 to 3 feet (0.3 to 0.9 m) tall

North American Range: Central and eastern Canada, central and eastern United States

Habitat: Open woodlands, prairies, meadows, and roadsides

Bloom Period: June to September

WOODLAND STRAWBERRY

(FRAGARIA VESCA)

Woodland strawberry is a small plant with flowers that turn into small, sweet, red strawberries. It has tiny white flowers with yellow centers and bright green leaves. Flowers have five petals and grow in clusters. Individual flowers are usually less than 0.5 inches (1.3 cm) wide. Compound leaves have three toothed leaflets. The plant spreads by sending out runners, which grow new plants nearby.

HOW TO SPOT

Size: 6 to 12 inches (15 to 30 cm) tall

North American Range: Canada, most of the United States, Mexico south to Guatemala

Habitat: Open forests, meadows, woodlands

Bloom Period: March to July

WHY ARE LEAVES GREEN?

Plant leaves are green because they contain a substance called chlorophyll. Chlorophyll helps plants absorb sunlight, which they use to make food. This process is called photosynthesis. Chlorophyll absorbs red and blue light from the sun but reflects green light, which makes leaves look green.

CAROLINA LARKSPUR

(DELPHINIUM CAROLINIANUM)

The Carolina larkspur is also known as the prairie or white larkspur. This slender, upright plant shoots up a spike that produces violet, blue, or white flowers. Each flower is about 1 inch (2.5 cm) wide with five petals that flare into a star shape. The larkspur has alternate leaves attached to a stem by short stalks. The leaves are compound, and each leaflet is deeply divided into five or more lobes. Short, soft hairs cover the larkspur's stem.

HOW TO SPOT

Size: 1 to 3 feet (0.3 to 0.9 m) tall

North American Range: Central Canada, central and southeastern United States, and northeast Mexico

Habitat: Prairies and dry open woodlands

Bloom Period: May to July

POISONOUS PLANTS

While plants in the genus *Delphinium* are delicate and beautiful, all parts of these wildflowers are toxic and should not be consumed by humans or animals. The plant contains diterpene alkaloids, natural compounds that can cause muscle weakness and even death. Dogs have been known to eat the plant's shoots and new leaves, where the compound is most concentrated. A common side effect is stomach pain.

COLORADO BLUE COLUMBINE

(AQUILEGIA CAERULEA)

The Colorado blue columbine is Colorado's state flower. The flower is about 2 to 3 inches (5 to 8 cm) wide. It has five blue petal-like sepals and five white inner petals. Each petal has a bit of blue near the base. Flowers that grow higher up in the mountains are usually a deeper blue. The plant grows in bushy clumps with multiple stems. The compound leaves have several leaflets that give a fern-like appearance.

HOW TO SPOT

Size: 1 to 2 feet (0.3 to 0.6 m) tall

North American Range: Montana south to Arizona and New Mexico

Habitat: Mountains, meadows, and moist woodlands

Bloom Period: June to August

COMMON BUTTERCUP

(RANUNCULUS ACRIS)

The common buttercup is also known as the tall buttercup. It is a tall plant with branching stems that are covered in fine hairs and alternating leaves. The plant's flowers are shiny and bright yellow. Each flower has five petals, yellow stamens, and a greenish center. Flowers are about 1 inch (2.5 cm) wide. The common buttercup is poisonous to humans and animals if eaten. Liquids from the plant can irritate the skin.

HOW TO SPOT

Size: 1 to 3 feet (0.3 to 0.9 m) tall

North American Range: Alaska, Canada, most of the United States

Habitat: Moist meadows, fields, and roadsides

Bloom Period: May to September

CREEPING BUTTERCUP

(RANUNCULUS REPENS)

The creeping buttercup spreads by growing along the ground and can form a dense ground cover. The plant's bright yellow flowers are about 0.5 to 1 inch (1.3 to 2.5 cm) wide and have five shiny petals. The compound leaves have three leaflets that grow in an alternate pattern on the stem. The leaves are covered with soft hairs.

HOW TO SPOT

Size: 0.5 to 2 feet (0.2 to 0.6 m) tall

North American Range: Alaska, Canada, most of the United States

Habitat: Meadows, marshes, roadsides, and other open areas

Bloom Period: May to August

MARSH MARIGOLD

(CALTHA PALUSTRIS)

The marsh marigold is also called cowslip. It has bright, shiny yellow flowers with five to nine petal-like sepals. The marigold's showy flowers are 1 to 1.5 inches (2.5 to 4 cm) across. The plant's leaves are thick, glossy, and heart or kidney shaped. Leaves often have wavy edges and alternate on the stem. The plant's branching stem is thick and hollow. This plant is toxic, and contact with skin can cause irritation.

HOW TO SPOT

Size: 1 to 2 feet (0.3 to 0.6 m) tall

North American Range: Alaska, Canada, northern United States

Habitat: Marshes, swamps, wet meadows, and along streams and brooks

Bloom Period: April to June

POLLINATION

Pollination is how flowers make seeds to grow new plants. It happens when pollen, a fine powder from a flower, moves to another flower of the same kind. Bees, butterflies, birds, and even wind help carry pollen from one flower to another. The animals that move pollen from one plant to another are called pollinators. Pollen from one flower must fertilize another flower in order for the plant to produce fruit and seeds.

PLANTAINLEAF BUTTERCUP

(RANUNCULUS ALISMIFOLIUS)

The plantainleaf buttercup is also called the meadow buttercup or water-plantain buttercup. It has small, bright yellow flowers that are about 0.5 to 1 inch (1.3 to 2.5 cm) wide with a waxy texture. Each flower has five green sepals, 4 to 14 petals, and a yellow to greenish center. The plant's shiny leaves are round or lance shaped. The plantainleaf buttercup can spread across a meadow and produce thousands of flowers.

HOW TO SPOT

Size: 1 to 2 feet (0.3 to 0.6 m) tall

North American Range: Western Canada, western United States, northwest Mexico

Habitat: Moist mountain meadows and muddy river and stream banks

Bloom Period: April to June

RUE ANEMONE

(THALICTRUM THALICTROIDES)

The rue anemone is a small plant that grows clusters of several white flowers, sometimes with a pinkish tinge. The flowers are about 0.5 to 1 inch (1.3 to 2.5 cm) wide and grow on short purple stems. Each flower has five to ten petal-like sepals and several greenish-yellow stamens. The plant's compound leaves have three lobed leaflets. The leaves grow in a whorl shape under the delicate flowers.

HOW TO SPOT

Size: 4 to 8 inches (10 to 20 cm) tall
North American Range: Ontario in Canada, central and eastern United States
Habitat: Open woodlands
Bloom Period: April to June

FUN FACT

Anemone flowers are named after the Anemoi, the Greek gods of the four winds, because wind carries the flowers' seeds.

SUGARBOWLS *(CLEMATIS HIRSUTISSIMA)*

Sugarbowls, also known as hairy clematis, are upright flowers that grow in clumps. The purple flowers are about 1 to 1.75 inches (2.5 to 4.4 cm) long and hang from the stem like a bell. The plant's cottony seeds grow in a seed pod inside the bell. The silverish-green compound leaves are hairy and divided into many lance-shaped lobes that grow in opposite pairs. The plant can be toxic if eaten.

HOW TO SPOT

Size: 8 to 12 inches (20 to 30 cm) tall

North American Range: Northwest and parts of southwest and central United States

Habitat: Grasslands, open pine forests, and sagebrush plains

Bloom Period: April to July

WILD COLUMBINE

(AQUILEGIA CANADENSIS)

The wild columbine is also known as the red columbine. Its striking flower droops like a bell. Each star-shaped flower has red sepals, yellow petals, and red spurs. Several long yellow stamens hang below the petals and sepals. The flower is 1 to 2 inches (2.5 to 5 cm) long. The plant's light green compound leaves have three leaflets that alternate on the stem.

FUN FACT

Wild columbine repels deer, making it an attractive plant for gardens.

HOW TO SPOT

Size: 1 to 2 feet (0.3 to 0.6 m) tall

North American Range: Central and eastern Canada, central and eastern United States, northeast Mexico

Habitat: Moist woodlands and open slopes

Bloom Period: April to July

WOOD ANEMONE

(ANEMONE QUINQUEFOLIA)

The wood anemone grows in large colonies in moist areas. It produces a single white 1-inch (2.5-cm) bloom with five to seven petal-like sepals. The sepals can have a pinkish hue on the underside. The wood anemone's flowers close in the evening, giving it the nickname nightcaps. The plant's compound leaves have three toothed leaflets that grow in a whorl pattern. The plant is toxic if eaten.

HOW TO SPOT

Size: 4 to 8 inches (10 to 20 cm) tall

North American Range: Central and eastern Canada, central and eastern United States

Habitat: Thickets, clearings, and woodlands

Bloom Period: April to June

FUN FACT

Ancient Romans believed wood anemones were lucky and could be used to prevent fever.

BITTERSWEET NIGHTSHADE

(SOLANUM DULCAMARA)

Bittersweet nightshade is also called climbing nightshade or deadly nightshade. Its drooping, star-shaped blue or violet flowers grow in clusters near the ends of branching stems. Each flower is about 0.5 inches (1.3 cm) across and has five petals and yellow stamens. Leaves are egg shaped, with smooth edges that taper to a pointed tip. Each leaf has two small lobes at the base. The plant produces a red, berry-like fruit. The plant's fruit and leaves are both poisonous if eaten.

HOW TO SPOT

Size: 2 to 8 feet (0.6 to 2.4 m) long
North American Range: Canada, United States, northwest Mexico
Habitat: Thickets and clearings
Bloom Period: May to September

Bittersweet nightshade fruit

BUFFALO BUR *(SOLANUM ROSTRATUM)*

Buffalo bur, also called horned nightshade, produces bright yellow star-shaped flowers with wavy edges and five tube-like stamens in the center. Flowers are about 1 inch (2.5 cm) wide. The hairy leaves have rounded lobes and smooth edges. The plant is covered in sharp, golden-yellow prickles, which led to its "bur" name. The plant is toxic if eaten.

HOW TO SPOT

Size: 1 to 3 feet (0.3 to 0.9 m) tall

North American Range: Alaska, Canada, United States, Mexico

Habitat: Edges of fields, roadsides, and other disturbed sites

Bloom Period: May to September

CAROLINA HORSE NETTLE

(SOLANUM CAROLINENSE)

Carolina horse nettle has star-shaped white flowers with yellow stamens in the center. The flowers are about 0.75 to 1.25 inches (2 to 3.2 cm) wide. The leaves are oval or egg shaped with wavy edges and shallow lobes. The plant is covered in prickly spines called nettles that help keep away predators. The plant's yellow fruit looks like a little tomato, but it is toxic if eaten.

Carolina horse nettle fruit

HOW TO SPOT

Size: 1 to 3 feet (0.3 to 0.9 m) tall

North American Range: Central and eastern Canada, United States, northern Mexico

Habitat: Fields, prairies, roadsides, and other disturbed areas

Bloom Period: May to October

COYOTE TOBACCO

(NICOTIANA ATTENUATA)

Coyote tobacco is sticky and covered with white hairs. Its pink or green tube-shaped flowers end in white lobes and are about 1.25 inches (3.2 cm) long. The flowers open at night to attract nocturnal insects and pollinators. The plant's lower leaves are oval shaped, while its upper leaves are narrower. Coyote tobacco was used by the Navajo people to treat headaches and other ailments.

HOW TO SPOT

Size: 2 to 5 feet (0.6 to 1.5 m) tall

North American Range: Western Canada, western United States, western Mexico

Habitat: Open, well-drained slopes

Bloom Period: May to October

GROUND CHERRY

(PHYSALIS HETEROPHYLLA)

Ground cherry, also called clammy ground cherry, grows bell-shaped flowers on branching, hairy stems. Each flower has greenish-yellow petals and a purplish-brown center and is about 0.75 inches (2 cm) across. Egg- or heart-shaped leaves are alternately attached to the stem. The leaf edges are lightly toothed. The plant produces a yellow berry-like fruit. The leaves and unripe fruit are poisonous, but the ripe fruit is often used to make jams and pies.

Ground cherry fruits grow within a green husk.

HOW TO SPOT

Size: 1 to 3 feet (0.3 to 0.9 m) tall

North American Range: Central and eastern Canada, central and eastern United States

Habitat: Dry woodlands, clearings, thickets, prairies, and disturbed areas

Bloom Period: June to September

JIMSONWEED *(DATURA STRAMONIUM)*

Jimsonweed is a vine that produces white or violet trumpet-shaped flowers that are about 2 to 4 inches (5 to 10 cm) long. The flowers open at night. The plant has large, dark green leaves that are egg shaped with irregular lobes or teeth. They are attached in an alternate pattern to the stem. The plant produces a fruit covered in spines, which is why the plant is sometimes called thornapple. Jimsonweed and its fruit are highly poisonous and can be fatal if eaten.

HOW TO SPOT

Size: 1 to 5 feet (0.3 to 1.5 m) tall

North American Range: Throughout North America

Habitat: Fields, barnyards, and other disturbed areas

Bloom Period: July to October

Jimsonweed fruit

FUN FACT

Jimsonweed is considered an invasive species throughout most of North America.

BIRDFOOT VIOLET *(VIOLA PEDATA)*

The birdfoot violet, or bird's-foot violet, has deep purple or blue flowers with orange stamens in the center. The flowers have five petals and are about 0.75 to 1.25 inches (2 to 3.2 cm) long. The leaves have three lobes that are deeply divided and splay out in a fan shape. The leaves grow near the plant's base. The leaves are arranged like little bird feet, which gives the plant its name. The plant's seeds produce a sugary gel that attracts ants, which carry the seeds to new locations.

HOW TO SPOT

Size: 4 to 10 inches (10 to 25 cm) tall

North American Range: Eastern Canada, central and eastern United States

Habitat: Open woodlands, prairies, fields, and roadsides

Bloom Period: March to June

COMMON BLUE VIOLET

(VIOLA SORORIA)

The common blue violet has purple or blue flowers with five petals and a white center. Flowers are about 0.75 to 1 inch (2 to 2.5 cm) wide. The plant has heart-shaped green leaves with wavy edges that grow near the plant's base. Common blue violets grow low to the ground and spread by seeds. The plant has been used in medicines. Its leaves are sometimes eaten in salads or cooked.

HOW TO SPOT

Size: 3 to 8 inches (8 to 20 cm) tall

North American Range: Central and eastern Canada, central and eastern United States, eastern Mexico

Habitat: Woodlands, meadows, and roadsides

Bloom Period: March to June

FUN FACT

The scent of a violet disappears after a few moments because the plant contains a compound that temporarily blocks a person from smelling it.

DOWNY YELLOW VIOLET

(VIOLA PUBESCENS)

The downy yellow violet is also known as the yellow forest violet. It has a small bright yellow flower with five petals. Its petals are covered in soft, fuzzy hairs like a bird's downy feathers. The lower flower petal is covered with purple veins. Each flower is up to 0.5 inches (1.3 cm) long. The plant's fuzzy leaves are heart shaped and alternate on the stem.

HOW TO SPOT

Size: 6 to 16 inches (15 to 41 cm) tall

North American Range: Eastern Canada, central and eastern United States south to Tennessee and North Carolina

Habitat: Woodlands and meadows

Bloom Period: May to June

WESTERN BLUE VIOLET

(VIOLA ADUNCA)

The western blue violet is also called the hooked-spur violet. Its colorful flower has five petals that are purple to blue with white near the base. Flowers are about 0.5 inches (1.3 cm) long. The leaves are primarily heart shaped with wavy edges, but some leaves are triangle or egg shaped.

HOW TO SPOT

Size: 2 to 4 inches (5 to 10 cm) tall

North American Range: Alaska, Canada, western and northern United States, northern Mexico

Habitat: Meadows, open woodlands, and roadsides

Bloom Period: April to August

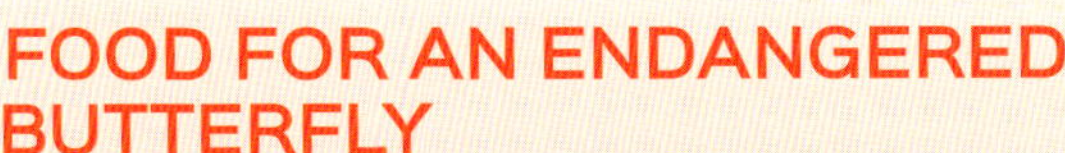

FOOD FOR AN ENDANGERED BUTTERFLY

The western blue violet is the only known host plant for the larvae of the Myrtle's silverspot, an endangered species of butterfly. The adult butterflies lay their eggs on the plant in June or July. In the spring the caterpillars feed on the leaves of the plant.

GLOSSARY

bract
A small leaf-like structure below a flower.

compound
Made of two or more elements.

disturbed area
Land that has been changed from its natural state.

invasive species
A non-native plant or animal that causes harm to native species when introduced to a new environment.

leaflet
The small part of a compound leaf.

lobe
A rounded or pointed projection on a leaf.

nectar
A sweet liquid released by flowers that attracts bees, butterflies, and other pollinators.

oblong
A long oval shape.

photosynthesis
The process in which plants use sunlight to make energy, or food.

pollen
A fine powder produced by plants for reproduction.

pollination
The transfer of pollen to allow fertilization.

rosette
A cluster of tightly packed leaves at the base of a plant.

salve
An ointment used to soothe or heal skin.

sepal
A modified leaf that forms the outer part of a plant's flower.

stamen
The male fertilizing organ of a flower.

tendril
A thread-like stem of a plant.

tepal
An outer part of a flower that is both a sepal and a petal.

thicket
An area thick with trees or bushes.

toothed
With a jagged edge.

toxic
Poisonous.

TO LEARN MORE

FURTHER READINGS

Carson, Mary Kay. *Tree, Wildflower, and Mushroom Spotting*. Macmillan, 2023.

Hart, Rachel C. *Poisonous and Deadly Plants*. Abdo, 2025.

Hoare, Ben. *The Secret World of Plants*. DK, 2022.

ONLINE RESOURCES

To learn more about North American wildflowers, please visit **abdobooklinks.com** or scan this QR code. These links are routinely monitored and updated to provide the most current information available.

PHOTO CREDITS

Cover Photos: Kristi Blokhin/Shutterstock Images, front (top left purple); Edgar Lee Espe/Shutterstock Images, front (top right lady slipper); Quang Ho/Shutterstock Images, front (upper left black eyed susan, bottom middle purple coneflower); Brian Woolman/Shutterstock Images, front (upper middle pink); Shutterstock Images, front (upper middle purple, upper right poppy, upper right more poppy, middle left white, middle right petunia, bottom right); Tony Baggett/Shutterstock Images, front (bottom left iris); Stephen B. Goodwin/Shutterstock Images, front (bottom left red); Tamara Kulikova/Shutterstock Images, front (bottom middle dark purple); Giedre Vaitekune/Shutterstock Images, back

Interior Photos: iStockphoto, 1 (top left), 1 (bottom left), 4 (bottom left), 4–5, 5 (top left), 5 (top middle), 5 (top right), 5 (bottom left), 5 (bottom middle), 7 (left), 7 (right), 11 (bottom), 12 (top), 15 (left), 15 (right), 16 (top), 16 (bottom), 17 (left), 17 (right), 18 (bottom left), 18 (bottom right), 19 (top), 19 (bottom), 20 (bottom), 22 (right), 23 (top), 24 (top), 24 (bottom), 26 (top), 27 (top), 27 (bottom), 28 (right), 30 (top), 31 (left), 31 (right), 32 (bottom), 33 (left), 36 (bottom), 39 (bottom), 40 (right), 43 (top), 44 (top), 44 (bottom left), 48 (top), 48 (bottom), 49 (right), 50 (right), 52 (bottom), 54 (top), 56 (right), 58 (top), 59 (top), 61 (bottom), 65 (left), 66 (top), 66 (bottom), 68, 72 (top), 72 bottom), 73 (bottom), 75 (top), 75 (bottom), 77 (bottom), 78 (bottom), 81 (bottom), 83 (bottom left), 83 (bottom right), 84 (top), 84 (bottom), 90 (right), 91 (bottom), 96 (top), 97 (top), 97 (bottom), 98 (top), 98 (bottom left), 98 (bottom right), 99 (top), 104 (right), 105 (bottom), 106 (bottom); Esin Deniz/Shutterstock Images, 1 (top right), 6 (right), 14 (right); Gerald Corsi/iStockphoto, 1 (bottom middle), 35, 59 (bottom right), 67, 80 (top), 91 (top), 93, 94 (right), 95 (bottom), 105 (top), 107 (left), 107 (right); Oleksandr Kostiuchenko/Shutterstock Images, 1 (bottom right), 33 (right), 103 (bottom); Shutterstock Images, 4 (top), 10 (left), 12 (bottom), 21 (top), 25, 38 (bottom), 39 (top), 47, 53 (left), 53 (right), 73 (top), 87 (left), 87 (right), 100 (right), 112 (left); Denise Hasse/iStockphoto, 4 (bottom middle), 63 (top); USFWS, 5 (bottom right); Kajdi Szabolcs/iStockphoto, 6 (left), 14 (left); Bob Didner/iStockphoto, 8; Ana Lopez Gacio/iStockphoto, 9; Tatsiana Maroz/iStockphoto, 10 (right); Robin Olimb/iStockphoto, 11 (top); Badra Adda Benattia/iStockphoto, 13 (top); Cristina Lonescu/iStockphoto, 13 (bottom); Dmitry Potashkin/iStockphoto, 18 (top); Alpamayo Photo/E+/Getty Images, 20 (top); Olga Strogonova/iStockphoto, 21 (bottom); USGS, 22 (left); Olya Solodenko/iStockphoto,

23 (bottom); Brian Woolman/ iStockphoto, 45 (top), 45 (bottom), 50 (left); Paul Wallén/ iStockphoto, 26 (bottom); Henk Hulshof/iStockphoto, 28 (left); Alan Schmierer/Flickr, 29 (top); Bettina Arrigoni/Flickr, 29 (bottom); Ladislav Kubeš/ iStockphoto, 30 (bottom); Veronique Monin/iStockphoto, 32 (top); Wikimedia Commons, 49 (left), 56 (left), 65 (right), 80 (bottom), 99 (bottom), 101 (left), 101 (right); NPS, 34 (left), 58 (bottom); Alex Manders/ iStockphoto, 34 (right); Carlos Martinez/iNaturalist, 36 (top left); Robert H. Mohlenbrock/ USDA, 36 (top right); Orest Lyzhechka/iStockphoto, 37 (top), 37 (bottom), 44 (bottom right); Luca Piccini Basile/ iStockphoto, 38 (top); Scisetti Alfio/Shutterstock Images, 40 (left); Lyudmyla Kharlamova/ Shutterstock Images, 41 (top); Goskova Tatiana/Shutterstock Images, 41 (bottom); Barbara Gabay/iStockphoto, 42 (left), 42 (right); Valeriy Shevtsov/ iStockphoto, 43 (bottom); Jeff Goulden/iStockphoto, 46 (left); Neal Herbert/NPS, 46 (right); Doug McGrady/Flickr, 51 (top); Dirk Daniel Mann/iStockphoto, 51 (bottom); iNaturalist, 52 (top); Mindaugas Dulinskas/ iStockphoto, 54 (bottom); Donna Bollenbach/iStockphoto, 55 (top), 70 (left), 70 (right), 94 (left), 104 (left); piemags/Nature/Alamy, 95 (top); Kathy Kafka/iStockphoto, 55 (bottom); Ken Wiedemann/ iStockphoto, 57; Murphy Shewchuk/iStockphoto, 59 (bottom left); Cecelia Alexander/ Flickr, 60 (top), 79 (right), 82 (bottom); Jason Hollinger/Flickr, 60 (bottom); Wolfgang Kaehler/ LightRocket/Getty Images, 61 (top); Inho Lee/iStockphoto, 62; Aimin Tang/iStockphoto, 63 (bottom), 96 (bottom); Anna Grigorjeva/iStockphoto, 64 (top); Nick Kurzenko/iStockphoto, 64 (bottom); Robert Winkler/ iStockphoto, 69 (top), 92; DP Wildlife Flowers/Alamy, 69 (bottom); Richard Bonnett/ Flickr, 71; Jeff Holcombe/ Shutterstock Images, 74 (left); Flickr, 74 (right); Siyue Steuber/ iStockphoto, 76; Ankur Mondal/ iStockphoto, 77 (top left); Harald Biebel/iStockphoto, 77 (top right), 112 (right); Bob Corson/ iStockphoto, 78 (top); David H. Kinder/NPS, 79 (left); Daria Chernoknyzhna/iStockphoto, 81 (top); David Cobb/Alamy, 82 (top); Michele Vacchiano/ iStockphoto, 83 (top); USFS, 85; Jasper Shide/Wikimedia Commons, 86; Sonnia Hill/Flickr, 88, 102 (top); Edward Snow/ iStockphoto, 89 (left); Gerald DeBoer/iStockphoto, 89 (right); Dirk Rietschel/iStockphoto, 90 (left), 112 (middle); Nurma Agung Firmansyah/iStockphoto, 100 (left); Helen Lowe Metzman/ USGS, 100 (bottom); Leila Dasher/iNaturalist, 103 (top); Allan Harris/iNaturalist, 102 (bottom); Sergi Vanovitch/ iStockphoto, 106 (top)

ABDOBOOKS.COM
Published by Abdo Reference, a division of ABDO, PO Box 398166, Minneapolis, Minnesota 55439.

Printed in China.
102025
012026

Editor: Kari Cornell
Series Designer: Colleen McLaren
Production Designer: Tara Raymo

LIBRARY OF CONGRESS CONTROL NUMBER: 2025939297

PUBLISHER'S CATALOGING-IN-PUBLICATION DATA

Names: Mooney, Carla, author.
Title: Wildflowers / by Carla Mooney
Description: Minneapolis, Minnesota: Abdo Reference, 2026 | Series: North American field guides | Includes online resources and index.
Identifiers: ISBN 9781098298975 (lib. bdg.) | ISBN 9798384932772 (ebook)
Subjects: LCSH: Wild flowers--Juvenile literature. | Flowers--Juvenile literature. | Plants--Juvenile literature. | Flora--Juvenile literature. | Encyclopedias--Juvenile literature.
Classification: DDC 582.1--dc23

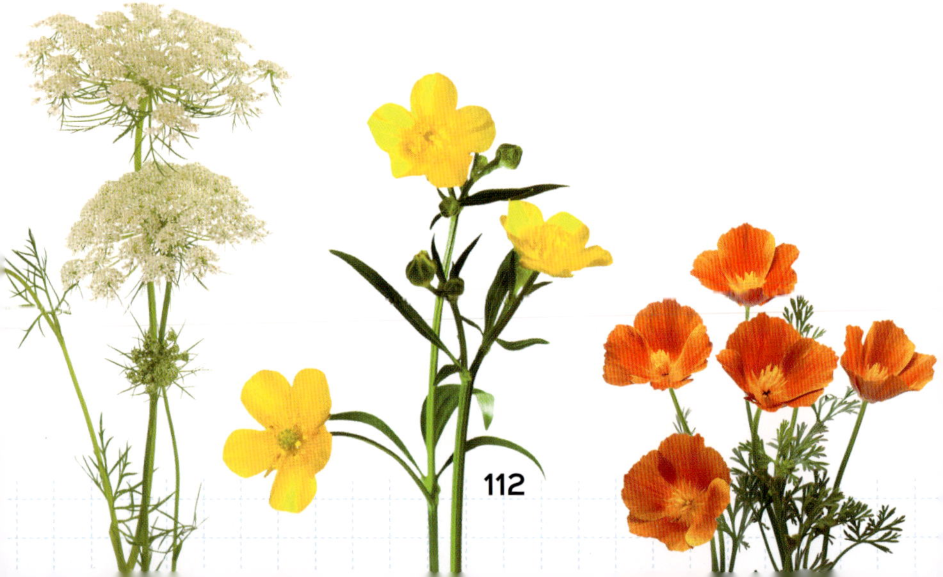